Dead on Arrival

This book is dedicated to the spirit of my grandmother,
Eva Tate,
and to the gift of her spiritual energy,
inherited by her female offspring,
and to my mother
Imani

Segun

Eva

Shanga

Oliver

in memory of my father
and to the awesome and wonderful support of
Judy Hogan.

Dead on Arrival

Jaki Shelton Green

[signature: Jaki Shelton Green]

Carolina Wren Press   Durham, North Carolina

Several of the poems in this book first appeared in the following publications: *Hyperion Poetry Journal, New England Anthology of Black Photography and Poetry, Harambee Report, The Chapel Hill Sun, Argos, Butt: A Quarterly, News of Orange County, The Loom, Out of Sight, If in the Beginning and I Had,* and *Sunbury Magazine.*

This publication is supported by a grant from the North Carolina Arts Council and was made possible in part through gifts to the Durham Arts Council United Arts Fund and support from the city of Durham.

Manufactured in the United States of America

Library of Congress Cataloging-in-Publication Data
Jaki Shelton Green, 1953–
Dead on Arrival
I. Title
PS3569.H39366D4 1983 811.54 83-15417
ISBN 0-932112-38-2 (pbk.)

Carolina Wren Press
120 Morris Street
Durham, NC 27701

The winged and delicate imagery of Jaki Shelton – the expression of an unusual emotional richness – may be a harbinger of poetic greatness. Take lines like these:

> "I remember . . . the
> few scattered peas . . .
> bleeding . . .
> with the sweat of their birthdust . . ."

or:

> "the beauty of yesterday
> becomes her shadow for growing
> out of my footprints."

The freedom of lines like these, their catching up a succulent freshness from her furrows, gives her poetry distinction. Brilliance is common, but that brilliance is unusual that is as natural as a thoughtless gesture of love.

And a sexuality unforced, unpostured, strong, rich, is frequent in her poetry:

> "those white shoulders have never
> locked
> around
> black thighs . . ."

She does not usually deal explicitly with race, as here, but the sensibility of the oppressed textures her work and gives it added dignity.

Her development, I trust, will be along her own idiosyncratic lines, along the lines of her originality; thus she will protect the fine freedom of her work. Should this idiosyncratic development continue, she will move, I believe, into a circle of greatness.

Lance Jeffers

PART I

Purpose

i am new
poem
i am new
woman
writing
poems
about life
about thunder
and about
fading dreams
i am new
poem
real new poem
fragments of black juju tales
fragments of seaweed
and dust
i am new poem
skipping and flying – giving life
leaving no marks.

perhaps you would like to plant
an acorn garden across my
shaven head

blood showers
beating into your stomach pit
becoming full
in your yielding folds.

my scalp will count the rests
inbetween your
        downpours
as you grow
        blood trees
        inbetween my folds.

to love a prince

let my hands bathe the crevices of your shadow
slipping into sensual, jeweled flesh
let my hands wait for your scent;
actions fertilize your laughter.
falling, rediscovering veiled promises
without touch of winter or source
    of your deepest rhythm.
    let it come in the form
    of thirst
    and in the form of truth.
let my tears gather close to your roots,
drowning your deepest seas
and possessing your slender waves.

nymph notes

i love you differently
as a concluding line
i have learned to
fear the sword of your
stare and the sound
of your closing eyes
and yet not enough
not enough
i have come to love you differently
while clouds surround your ears
and rain knots
bind my feet beneath
your thighs
steady beneath your thighs
i could learn to love you differently
if only you would remove the rain.

for my sisters

We sat embraced,
interlocked within
the pains of our
restless beings
we sat giving
into the wombs of truth
new blessings
but sewn into old rituals
we sat giving
the blood
and waste of sacrificial honor
while our spirits
were rising and melting
into sun-lit
love spasms…

to the brother who got over with my shadow
or travels to the corner

there is nothing to knock up
there is nothing to knock up
                knock up
                knock up
                knock up
        lock up pain
there is nothing to knock up
there is nothing to knock up
mother knock up pain
mother knocked out of pain
pain out
                lock up
                knocked up in pain
                mother.wife locked
                knocked
pain knocked in locked up mother
wife knocked pain in lock up
                lock in
                lock up
                pain in knocked up wife
                locked in
                locked in
                locked in
there is nothing left to lock up
there is nothing left to knock up
pain is locked up.mother. wife.knocked up.

TODAY is the same day as your yesterday
        today like last night and i have not
        written a single poem
        i have not kissed away the silent screams of
        death-filled day
        i have not answered the pure questions about
        black tomorrows or commented on your fading
        beauty although, strangely as it may seem i have
        decided to give birth, give you a framed tear-drop
        for good fortune, travel south to the love doctor,
        seek out the right herb for the right pain, and
        somehow continue to open the curtain to the sun,
        improvise that i am a cosmic angel, smile when you
        scream and understand the warmth that is lost in
        a blizzard. and all the time i will continue to conjure
        your spirits, engulf your manhood and rest hoping
        that tomorrow i will not have to write an excuse
        for having not written a poem.

the moon is a rapist

why do you kneel there peeing in my window
you kneeling there upon my earth
impregnating the night crawlers with glow
their bodies do glow
as your soft yellowness penetrates my walls
you entered as you were
yellow streams of pee
leaving traces upon the bed
rapist you are
beating your rays into my buttocks
setting my breast aflame
moon babies i shall abort
moon babies come out of my birth pouch
soft rapist leaving me as the
sun knocks loudly upon my door.

to the lady of the house

the only place for you
is your backyard
where the grass refuses
to kneel to the rain
and your flowers
send kisses to the sun.
in the mornings
your house seals away
the questioning echoes of loneliness and grief
while rainbows of solitude
paste themselves across
your ceilings.
we come to your house
with the seasons
snow and sun
and the thunder of our
offspring.
and there in your backyard
we find you
scolding the dust that
refuses to settle evenly.

But don't let me hear that bed squeak

light bright
bodies tight
moonlight
sweet passionate
wet flight
and from across the hall
the aged woman echoed
you can hug and kiss
and get wet,
sweat and rub and
pull all you want to
but don't let me hear
that bed squeak

black mothers somehow always knew
the thoughts
the wetness
the truth inside of
sound in flesh sound
wet sound
ageless sound
ritualistic
of ancient movement.

on your way to an od

when i was ten
you were seventeen
already halfway a man
i was a straight
ninety-five minus many pounds heavy
i wore braids long enough to wrap to the front and chew
for which i got my butt popped many times
and grandma was the butt popper
she even popped me for cutting up the sunday paper
but i simply couldn't help it
you had scored twenty-three points for central high
even the white folks knew your picture meant business
i cut out your picture with grandma's fishing hook
i slipped into aunt alice's school glue and
so here you are plastered to my baby doll's stomach
grandma won't find you here and even if she did
she'd just pop me and say lawd knows girl i don't know
what yo mama gonna do wit you
you would have liked me at ten
even some of the big boys used to run me home from
                                                the store
i guess i was kind of cute but i was really afraid
to really look at myself in a mirror
cause every time mama caught me in the mirror
she tell me one of them stories bout some woman
long time ago who stayed in the mirror so much
that she got so pretty that couldn't nobody stand her
mama couldn't stand being around nobody who was so dumb

they couldn't po piss out of a boot
but i still know you would have really liked me
me being the bright little child that i was
but are you listening now
do you care that your picture got torn off the doll
do you care that central high was burned down by some
evil crackers evil crackers evil crackers
i know you don't care and i don't care either
i cried when i read about you going to school in maryland
mama and all the older folks were talking about how good
you was looking in sunday school sunday and how proud
miss effie should be to have a nice christian boy like you
but i didn't tell em' bout the time we was in the back
of uncle ervin's store and you was messing with me
naw i didn't tell em i swear i didn't
yeah you was a good good boy
tasting wine and playing spin the bottle with them girls
from up the road
i didn't even tell em bout that time when you was in church
and them women was taking communion you and artis bright
was peeping under they dresses with a mirror
but are you listening now
and am i really here
are you really kissing my toes sending
rainstorms to the top of my head
are you really inside of me creating more BB stars
creating creating
but there will be no central highs for them
are you listening as you od od od
are you listening are you listening
as you go as you go riding high riding high

there was a needle in my child's arm this morning
the sunday's sport column read,
"1967 star at C.H.S. dies of over dose"
and i taped that picture to my child's grave

midsummer dream or coming of the nemesis

the clouds turned away
rushed hiding with grey disgust
the sun tilted its body
and rose higher
cursing birds and sobbing repulsively
steel hands reached
across the sky
reddened the distant heavens
and slapped the eyes
with past present future
alone in the place
that is remembered as no place
all stems all leaves
such strange fruit
steel hands froze the head
and coming rain
sliced the kneaded skull
like Missouri hands at sunrise
black love
black dresses black octobers
see. the head falls evenly with
bourgeois loveliness
spirited breast
scream i am i am
and alone marry the
blood
as glimmering; flowered
winged things
crawl along the virgin

face.
the sun dangled a gold
pendulum in the East
straight as an arrow
arranging the oiled death bed
such cold, cold
truths
seven slender fingers
rise out of the glass
and spread out the ivory arms
touch the exquisite skull
and leave under the strings
of winter.
wasted spirit
in nightgown
afraid of bees and butterflies
as they float inside
the sun's wounds
eating the toasted pollen
the steel hand
offers flowers to suck
designs sweet tribal markings
above the eye
and corrects my kissing
corrects my smiles
coils into my mouth
and waits to season this flesh.
while jewels, dancing above the calm,
are consumed in triumphant
psalms.

i want to give you me
as a river
streaming
flowing with richness
with teardrops forming
glaciers in your body
giving wet substance
to your wet form.

i want to give you me
as a flooding lake
dissolving all solid forms
giving up and giving back
i want to give you me
swallowing your tears
burying your succulent treasures

the loss of me

you say you don't need me
you have even said on special occasions
get the hell out of my life
and somehow my suicide became a ritual.
i cried when you discovered me sprawled upon the waves
making endless love to sea phantoms below
i cried even when you tried to wipe away my death smile.
i felt the empty shock that froze you as you gave me back
to the sun, the air, the water, the fires of my beginning.
i even measured your heartache so it would fit into my
                                    dust mound
and now that i have become an expression of your artistic
                                    moods
it is really time for me to live this poem.
   i be like a mistress to the sea
   seducing the air and the wind
   they do not turn over and sleep
   they grant me my fullness
   allow me to soar high
        to become full
        impregnated with sealife
        a fetus claimed by the air.
   i can give life to the darkness.

song of david
            for jon

    soft red circles spin
            before your lips
        cups that have tasted beauty
        shapeless lips forming love
        lips that have tasted poison
        and enjoyed its fire.
                i counted the circles
                between your toes
                    seven
                        full
                            with moonstone.
seven soft red circles spin and spin
            into your eyes
            put out the fire
        consume the moonstone
                and paint your lips.
you are a soft red circle
wrapped around my lungs
        (all your dreams come true)
            paint your lips
            swallow my peace
dance the dance
sing the song
                the spirits sing
wrap into my shoulders and cry
wrap into my breasts and praise
the dance is the witness to your truth.
a thousand red circles smile in your kisses.

moon lady
  hoists her body
    above your shoulders
     and you
      dive in
        never to
          know sleep
           again
        to forever live
          perpetual day

moon shadows
  draw red circles
    around your soul
      your voice smiling, fades into a
      soft mellow
        black high
      you go on singing
        never knowing night
        never closing your mouth.
  now, i lay me down to sleep
  I pray the lord my soul to keep
  come on catch me if you can,
floating on a black high
  how high are the clouds purple lady,
How close to night are you.
Red circles
    lock
    lock tight
  around your moon mistress
open your legs wide
  i want the night.

dust memoirs

candles drip air
washed away smiles linger to breathe;
a skeletal interpretation of motherhood
suspends itself above penurized nativity.
go into yourself and free those
midsummer visits free those grasshopper tragedies;
free those public telephones with passionate coffin smells
drip into your burial urn.drip.
this is called neurotic fiction.iamgoingoutofmyselfintoa
woman without skin,into a face without a mouth, into
a woman without a man i am woeman.woeman.this is
neurotic fission.drip, drip into my confusions. i am
vaguely alive,am dying alive native depression and
intellectual inclinations balance this head.keep it adrift.
i have no sweet songs of georgia pine to sing. i have no
succulent verse of carolina wind to whisper. i have only
come to bury my dead.i have only come to bury my dead.
this is my only sonnet.write in the dust with or without
the sandman's help...the moon is late.is somewhere raging
suicides and spreading apart skies.such is a product of my
unconsciousness. i do not know who i am and why i
choose...life? the writing will actualize the deed the
writing will fire the first plunge and sink the first little dove
into painless death.

ii

it is the night that has decided to bring to me such taste.
such deafening shrills of roses awakening, even the earth
has danced around this bed,has whispered its wishes of
good luck. has called out to the sun to be obedient to its

lost father, to its wounded earthgod.kneel and receive.
it is the night that caresses the past and arouses its
haunting sport.doves of cocained misery fly into this bed,
offer gifts to this rich life root and kill themselves in the
shadow of day.

iii

something still continues to open my head step inside and
dance with crooked swords. still as the black nights that has
recently decided to swallow birds and men whole that
stuffs the music of captivity inside my soul and compels
me to sing slave lyrics. a natural man of woe:woe man.
spitting dust into clean beds.spitting death into loose
lungs.playing broken keys inside sweaty seeds. sweaty
seeds about to germinate with bones.sticky bones grow
inside my lungs,pierce up through my head.blossom into
blood trees.blood seeds.coming down, coming out like
pieces of a dead woman's tongue, burned white.alive.
with darkness.dead birds buried in fleshy rivers, tear open
their thick bowels and balance each new clap of thunder.
bones and hearts and august sky. burn together in celestial
bosoms.

PART II

and in my old days — when my spirit is ripe they shall
call me *mmeda* — meaning "it has never come before."

agoliagbo!
agoliagbo!
do not try to
renew me
i am fluid
beyond
clear
bubbling
tides
i am fluid
do not try to
possess me
dance
with
my language
and sing
with
my rhymes
do not try to hold me
i am fluid
half river/half cloud
choked
out of a young valley
shadow
of
a deepening sky

do not breathe
me deeply
i split
into
hours
and sink
into shores
i am fluid
i want sky
hands on sky
do not
come near.

night queen inheriting the silence of night. the silence of dead shadows pierce and break my dance. the room becomes liquid. runs into my thick bones and i listen to its echo. i listen to all the people i love, walk, embarrassed, laugh at their thin frail emptiness. i feel lost and walk through the streets like weather. i move my fingers over his face and they burn, scorched with pain, truth. get rid of your words lady, he once said. But i am myself. fill up your mornings with afternoons. rip truth to shreds.

my mornings have become tinted with brutal motion. brutal dance giving blood to the sunrise. i touch his face again. this time it is satin. sweet. calm. but i have loved all the people i can love. thin morning sweat covers my skin. Shivers my woman wetness. i don't want to sit waiting for his poems to accuse me. i don't want to read poetry, sing sonnets, dance with funk while my friends die. to your question, i answered, no, i've never fucked in spanish. i've never known midnite truth. this woman wants to die. i will not smother her, i will give her back to foreign men in unnamed cities who all chant her name in seven different lingos. they already dig her grave and harvest roses for her dark face. i will not smother into the silence of her screams.

the foreign men sleep.

it is done.

it is done.

the lies creep up into you like the dust smooths itself across the river. you light another cigarette. curse me sharply in french.

if the walls were men, would they plot your death? take off your face. the shadow is more beautiful. your

eyes have grown wings and flown away several times.
your lips become stone, shrinking innocent cries.

the musician hits notes at random. creates music by
accident. i again walk the streets like weather while black
notes form around my face. believe them, they are real.
they are thin, fragile, absorbing the whiteness of the sky.
remembering my face, remembering the foreign men.
they play a death melody. you are more beautiful than
before he said. and i came again before disappearing into
the dance, the weather, the foreign men. the foreign men
disintegrating into my black skin. i remember each face
before it died. before the breathing stopped. before the
morning turned cold. i fasten their bones inside my mouth
and write postcards to America's insanity. another man
walked thru me. creates pictures of foreign crying children.
i scream hard and swallow him fast. i write more letters, this
time to intelligent night spirits who will always remember.

and she died. and she died.

i have loved all the people i can. the poet. the
musician. the full moon lady. the neruda prayer boys. the
dying child inside me. i have loved all the people i can
and you still come.

and you can still feel.

your wetness burns inside me. the rain smells funny.
the rain smells like me. i continue pouring myself into
you. you continue to drink cold color. i must write more.
i walk to the window and curse the rain. they all sit robed
in polyester disgust. they all sit with the taste of flesh
inside their tongues. they sit. the white men and they
wait. their polyester collapses and they are lost outside to
full moons. fine black women eclipse their paths like

birds, and the foreign men — return — walk around them, suspended in slow motion. headless. they all come dressed in clean white warmup suits. the black angels present weapons and sink into thin pockets. before you kiss me see what you can see. your eyes. linked to the white suits. no, i've never fucked in spanish.

must people stare at his paintings. his poems, his dying woman. pull the curtains quick. there is a river giving birth inside. there is a moon. the father waiting impatiently.

to fear the beginning is much more. to fear my color is a pure act. a clean act. the foreign men clap and offer blind gifts.

i touch his face again. this time his paintings smile and i take his dying seriously. you are emptying me again. i am replaced by brown greasy bags and you eat all the fingers inside. you eat all the fingers inside. your paintings cry and your woman dies but the foreign men will not come. they are afraid of the sun. they are afraid of the egyptians. the warm light burns them. i am a pure image, learning to fuck in spanish. learning to recognize your pain. your smell has become the rain. thick with winter. i want to touch her hair, but lower my hands again to your face. burned again. you sleep during the day while i choreograph funeral marches inside the bedroom. the weeping foreigners sleep with you under your ugly breath.

i'll die on the street one morning with the sun pulling apart my thighs, with the air peeling away my underwear. i'll die beneath your polyester factories with the nakedness of my breast turned east. beside a river with old cars still smoking with anne's cough. her final cough. beside the abandoned cement yard with old ovens wiping sylvia's sweat from their doors. beside you with my naked nymph shadow begging for forgiveness. Neruda designed simple dances for fresh girls in white muslin to perform. i crawl into sylvia and wait. i am perfect rivers. swollen with myself. i die silently sandwiched between winter and life. there are letters to write, prayers to be danced. wet cement locks around me a winter wall. i freeze like a perfect pencil. a sharp tip to be sliced off. frozen. unable to keep the shadows out of my eyes. unable to reach down to my female house. unable to soothe my back and suck at my own nakedness. the cement wall laughs and shatters itself into the darkness of your eyes. the swallowed fingers rust inside your stomach. your telephone rings. it is a telegram from America.

all your women are dead. your mother died inside the smell of the foreign man. all your children laugh. come back to your segregated bathroom at once. don't worry. it is vogue, chic to hate foreigners. we'll wait for your train. see you friday. love, the chains of peace.

Lady, forget your poems. Lady, you always called me Lady. Lady come feel my tall shadow.

come drink life with me.

Lady, come dance under the moon with me. Lady, give up. leave Sylvia alone. stop tickling Anne. Stop it lady. lady if I laugh i'll cough up the fingers. Lady, there are seven foreign men at the door. Lady, you fuck so well in spanish.

it is raining

    it is raining here as i dial the last three digits
    to your number
    i listen to the eight
    dead rings
    echo into my ear
    and imagine your tossing, reaching for the lost rings
    inside the room
    and finally your whisper covers the dead.
Hello, you whisper with an apologetic cough
i pause
silence
hello, louder
more desperate
i detect from your breathing
you have a cold
and i make mental note –
rosehip tea
scold you for not addressing
yourself
to the winter.
my thoughts are scattered
you are still
whispering hello.
    i remember i have not spoken.
    you are relieved to hear a voice
    my voice?
    and your prelude
    "is something wrong"
    It's three in the morning "here", you say.

What time is it
and my silence
makes apologies
— again i've forgotten the
eight hour time difference.

i hurl paper fish through your window
they land on the bed
and you brush them under the covers
under the covers.

you remember to ask
about the children
the job
the car
the rent
and finally the writing
the poetry,
and i cry heavily
while you tiptoe
to your kitchen
stretching the thin
umbilicus
of our relationsip.
i know the movement
am aware
of the refrigerator opening
the yogurt top
popping onto the counter.
i wonder if you remember

to water the plants i
bought for your
bathroom shelves.
i cry harder
i already feel their
death in your voice
your nervous morning movement.
a dance.
      i snatch the phone
      from the wall and imagine
      it is your head
      being snatched
      and
      i want to remove
      the smile
      and
      the open eyes.
      i watch the phone:
         it smiles back

monday in november

nice to be alone with the roar of your smiles
the cool whispering chant of your kisses
Southern
organic
man
　　　　with the currents of a thousand rivers
　　　　running through you.
　　　　my fingers become naked
and dance alongside your neck.
sunset overtook morning
and the rain
　　　　left us
　　　　reaching
　　　　touching
　　　　　　　　i'll come back.
deep morning blues
　　　　coming
　　　　　　　　to break the news.
you left me
　　　　sitting,
　　　　　　sprawled over a mud ditch
　　　　　　facing west.
i placed your shadow back into the closet.
i removed the soiled sheets
burning them separately
　　　　behind the clocks of time.
　　　　spinning away.
　　　　trying to weave you into

a red clay mound.
           trying to give your darkness color.
trying to unfold the last page from your book of dreams.

your voice slices my fingers and they
    fall
    evenly
    into the flowers
                       roses, your gift to me.
i walked back into your shadow's box
    and promised to not smoke in bed
    to not do coke alone
    and to always water the plants.
                   i remembered the trip
                   when i went away,
i remember the empty bean pods lying in the sun
and the few scattered peas
           bleeding
           with the reflection of their growth
           with the sweat of their birthdust.
you moved my feet
                   faster
                   to the car. i kept remembering
all the abundant,
           huge,
           suicides i had committed
           near the lake
                   on the porch
                   under the rain
                       by the church.
           all the suicides

and i laughed
then cried.
i remembered the place
where babies grew
and men died.
your warm
moist bed
was the biggest mirror
i'd ever known.
i'd love to take it home under my shirt
or
seal it away
in a prism
of skin.
you just insert it here
and close your eyes.
and i swallowed hard
and all
the round cowboys
began to cry
and suffocated
against my bigness.
i loved the clouds and the leaves
and the brown words that tripped over your smile.
i grew to watch
myself
watching
you and became good
at it. quite nice.
my natural privilege was to lock
you away in

                    white wilderness
          Great
          Great
          with insects defending the valleys.
lock you away
          inside tidal moods
          and nurture your appetite for morning
          i feed you
          poems
sprinkled
               with gold.
               there
               there is your smell again
               aching
               in the bed
               with dark
                         dead lovers
                         to
                              release
                         the calm
and make your breath precious
                              again
                              returning
                              to
                                   empty mouths
                              as mother
                              as baby.
the shadow between us
          decides
               where the tension
               will surface.

            the mask
                begins to melt
                and runs
                            into your pillow.
the unborn present
                contracts
                again. carrying you away
                to the where place
                of the records
                    of time. of lovers who have
                    forgotten to make love
whose eyes sleep
while
        their bodies
        roam
        and
        dance.
        whose voices are replaced
        by those of dead tribes.
i walk in the moonlight
but they don't speak
                        of my rambling spirit
                        anymore.
    they have taken away
                the house
                the dope
                the children
                the land
                the blood.
    they forget the writer woman
    with the four candles for legs.
    they remember her belly

        and how on
                        wednesdays
                        she stuffs her thighs
                        with rosemary leaves
                        and swells up
                        like winter
fresh with
        wind sperm.
                they remember her belly that bears
and drops stars into baskets
                        i weave more songs
                        inside her basket
                                and close my eyes.

                        *   *   *

i was raised
in the air
sprouted
from exotic
moon
shadows
whisper thin
midnights
(a cast illusion)
dramatic shivering
motion/quivering
like dark men
in dark suits.
i was a solid
breath
translated
into miniature forevers.

december

        i wore you tight
        like the skin fastens
        itself to the burn
            to the fire
            the rich
            ripe red.

i wore you tight
tight as the funeral glove
that holds the widow
and squeezes her pain.
tight inside of my womb.
polished and smoothed your
wet-smiles.
i even wore the smile of a
woman in pain, lost the glove,
found the dead man burning leaves
on top of Mt. Fear.
too fast to be a little girl they said.
too mean to be a lady
stripping berries and tree bark and
collecting roots in pots, going to boil
out your name.
going to boil your name
then write in red
your name on a green sheet. wash it in the sweat
of a four day de-virgined boy.
sleep on the green sheet with
devirgined boy for six nights

7th night wash your hands in the blood
from his lips.
    i wore you tight
    like the skin fastens
    itself to the burn
      to the fire
      the rich
      ripe red.

to the man in the door
    (at the window/sometimes you)

you come everyday
briefly
stealing
with your eyes
wrapped away
sealed
in still
damp tissue
inside moist
pockets.
the sheepskin
sewn
across your eyes
has begun to loosen
little snow birds
wait
for real snow
to melt
and bring
back
the blood.

sunday breakfast / in between fears

your fingers end here.
the fierce seeds of spring
must now be spread through
me by the trembling hands
of the wind.
your fingers end here.
it is beyond
the white of the snow
and yet contained in
the soles
of your feet.
     the sky runs with me
     toward the mirrored
     sun's reflection
     over the veil
     of sea mist –
     over the silenced fog
     into
     the shade of my memory.
     love pains
     that forever
     drift
     downstream
     liquid moons
     reaching down
     to join
     the dance.
the sun pulls me into another direction.
the beauty of yesterday

becomes her shadow growing out
    of my footprints.
my sprouting seeds take form.
my limbs dance for rain
liquid protection
weaving knives
in and out
of my womb.
a beautiful way
to possess
a beautiful man
to sweat
ánd
pour out
fragrances
of
pulsating
fertility.

shadow

those white shoulders have never
locked
around
black thighs
those chrome teeth
never tasted
and sealed
in the throat
the thick sweetness
of black sweat.
those white hands
never
painted truth
inside this
red womb
never removed
history
never knew
the true
meaning
of TCB
or the
sweet
splendor
in a black woman's smile.

note to a dark girl

i slip into black houses slip out of black slips black lace
black pearls and slip under your black fire burn into silvery
black rose buds slip into your skin and begin to sew up
black holes black hurt spots slip into black muscles and
realize that black bones hold up the mythical universe give
back black strength through black kisses and experience
black desert love. Experience unpoisoned black languages
unphotographed black breasts possessed by black babies
to listen and survive off black breath black discovery
heavy with black voices praying to black angels singing
black poems inside black nights black womb infused with
dark sperm nightmare black nightmare again black baby
black death black hunger black poems to fill the womb
black wind to guard against the rain black angels to cause
black salvations black springs black female child promising
life.

love abortions

i sit inside the galvanized tub
with the heat leaving the water.
the heat beginning its ritual
pilgrimage
up through my womb
to swirl and twist
and finally ooze
into the bed place
where we slept
into the dark womb
room of our visitations.
the water begins its task.
the witches come
while my eyes are locked
and paint white circles
under my eyes,
around my neck
and create
glass bracelets for my breast.
i awaken as the first one
begins
to stuff the legs
and arms of the child
into white bags,
the second seals and sanctions
this wedding with the flames
from the third candle
tied around her waist.
they lock my womb again

as the last drop of water
crawls out and becomes
vaporized
in my blood
they lock my womb
and tie the bag
round my thighs
twice
twice
twice
tying twice
to keep out
the evil.
to sanction their suicides.

getting to know you
is listening
to the deafening
tic tic
of the clock, pretending that your arrows do not scare me
because i am an *artiste*
pretending that the sound
of your silence
is another wet pillow
and my eyes
march past the rain.
past your deathly arrows
i am an *artiste*
offering you
sacred tears
and golden breasts.
    a tear rolled down my cheek
    your dance becomes more
    violent. a silver mist
    rained on you and you held me close
    closer than the blue
    clings to the sky. closer than the
    sun moves in rhythms.
    your movements
    become circles.
    you took your woman
    tonight
    love haunts your bones
    hot flesh
    surrounds
    this woman creation

that your eyes
stab
and bury
in colored beads.
a taste of honey
to sanction
this arrival.
a black book closes
on another chapter.
     free to return
     to your smiles
     your promises
     kisses
     and perhaps
     even the sun.
     free to return to the eyes
     and wait there
until
the dance
is only
a tremble.
only a rumble.
     the night sounds cover me
     i reach into the wind
     echo night whispers.
     i have cried
     because
     the night is cold
     the wind is full
     of your breath

you become an air
spirit and alone
harness my fear.
        the leaves tell me
        i must eat
        pure food
        walk only on dirt roads.
        swim in dust pools
        perhaps i will find
        my skin again
        perhaps i will return
        to your trembling
        bed
        and learn a different fear.

overheard

magic twine woman
wrap your pores
inside me
knot me into
organic kiss-juice
    kissjuice
    magic twine
    woman
    knot my tongue
    kiss my knees
    until they break.

* * *

for minnie ripperton

    there is room
    for your bones
        of jade
        and jointed strength
        for your touchless
        desire
        and bare fears.
    there is room
    to clothe you
    and calm
    enough
    to haunt you.

i have forgotten exactly
what time in what city
or what sunset
my pain began
i have remembered
to forget
what man
chose not to speak to
the light
chose not to allow
the sunlight
to enter
and caress
my other breast
Jealous mornings
i have forgotten
what it is like to
wake up without
name
without poem
without pain
and turn over to face the sun.
what room
does this act take place in
into whose
grave
do i allow
these bones
to crawl
into. what woman
will I
cease to
return to.

i have begun to see the rain
through vinyl pupils
and watched it
spread
      like the wings
      of twenty beetle bugs
i have tasted snow
while my tongue
still sucked wax
from the left side
of honey combs
my hair
lifts up into the stars
and each strand
becomes
a comet
becomes
a fleeting
light world. i have begged for rain tastes
and prayed for snowstorms
inside my ears.

eagerly

a naked
cosmic
moon
lingers and drifts
between my
legs
twitching
blossoming
into some
silkened
blackness
black roses
sweet breath
of cool
summer
a bouquet
of wetness
a rich rare
rose.

beyond my lips
is the untouched
music
of dark nights. my dreams
explode into
weeping, trembling songs.

the moon plans to bury me

I.

the moon plans to bury me
   (when i was
        younger
        they called
        me
        a beautiful
        black
        flower)
he has already
covered my arms
legs,
thighs
   with
        the trembling
        waters
        of winter
        and spring's
          union
        (i was a loud
        guiding galaxy
        full of naked sun
        drowning in
        rhythmic games)
the moon is caressing
my dreams
flashing smiles

back into
the sky
flashing my first
rhythms
above graves (i chant into soft ears
                paint rainbows inside tongues

II.

my spiritual smiles
kiss your
thundering
wisdoms
become
whole inside
your footsteps
the moon plans to
   bury me
   past
   all barriers
   of light
   of light-life
   vibrant
   raw.
   thirsty
   life-life loves light
the moon plans to
     bury me
     wrap me up in
     a golden

             breast
             wrap me up into
             a warm
             child
             inside
(big, strong sunsets) a warm
                        womb.
(it takes a long time for
     my veins to flow).

III.

the moon plans
to bury
me
swollen
blue
with poet-juice
inside my
teeth
between my
legs
wrapped
around
my head
upstream
up sky
up hell
up heaven
up Place

no place
the moon
is my
verse
cutting
between my
rhythms
black love
buried.

(when i was young
i cried about dreams that might come true)

IV.

the moon plans
to bury
me
soak under
my grave
and collect
my bones
sell them
to the juju
man
and i sleep
softly
beside
black fruits
black juju

beads
black dreams

VISIONARY RAPE
the moon
stole my first
poem
for the juju
man
who turned it into
a scarf
for his wife
my first poem
a grease rag
for the juju lady

V.

dust
dust
i cough dust into
my first poem
that ran off
to the moon
the growing moon
smiling
and teasing
making
blood
freeze

making my
poem
a cloud
for old souls
to rest upon.
my dark wings
coated
with
dust
begin to
fall begin
to soften
and melt
into the night.
swallowed whole with light

dead on arrival
for judy hogan

the leaves smiled and gathered
close to the water;
the black birds flew too high
and became air.
her
hand fell limp
beside the stretcher
and they all asked
her name.
they asked me to identify
the smile.
the smell
the style of her art.
they asked for identity
a season.
a year.
a place.
i could only give them
the time of birth
her astrological chartings
and the names of her lovers
but they wanted
a name
a stock number
a style symbol.
i could only speak of her
mother
and her sisters

and her daughters.
they dressed the hand
in a white glove
and sewed it
inside her womb
clenched
with the names
of all the people
she'd borne.

PART III

a man reaches out to me
drops his head in my lap
and wants me to fly.

a man reaches out to me
drops his head in my
lap and i sprout wings
a man reaches out to me
drops his head in
my lap and i touch clouds.
a man reaches out to me
drops his head in
my lap and i
breathe rain.

* * *

if i were the creator one
i'd line this womb mouth
w/rose water
that sweetens your tongue
and quenches your birth thirst
i the creator one
would shine through
winter eclipse
winter sun
moving across
the map of this broad stomach
continent. this round globe of
flesh, cell, tissue, smiles, fusing
creating another star.

Masks

i have worn masks
black
white
red
dead
alive
whispers
tears
i have worn masks
those come-here-baby-and-look-at-me MASKS
those
do-you-wanna-dance
Masks
those
PLEASE-DON'T-STOP MASKS
those Don't-Touch-Me MASKS
those catch-me-if-you-can
masks
those no-no-no
masks
those three-o'clock-i-can't-sleep-where-is-my-man MASKS
those I-don't-want-to-go
masks
those please-please-please masks
those baby-i-been-good masks
those monday morning
smile-your-ass-off-please-be-kind-to-the-white-folk
Masks
those Friday night empty

Masks
those torn masks
those hurt masks
i have worn masks
swollen full of history
masks
i have worn masks
crossing rivers
those please-hurt-me,-
i-like-to-bleed masks
those half-white-birth
masks
those real masks
those brother-can-you-ever-
stop-playing-the-blues masks
those sunday-morning-
can-i-sing,-can-i-choke-out-the-lord's-prayer masks.
i have worn masks
touched masks
face masks
tongue masks
those ape-like
rape-me-again masks
i-have-known-new-england-
in-the-winter masks
ICE MASKS
sweat fire masks
i have known red
masks full of lip
poison full of sister-
kiss-me mask

MASKS I HAVE
WORN
hard, coarse, erect
Masks
masks
Masks. faces. western mask
behind Obatala loveliness
i-know-faces. i-touch masks
i-touch-face.
i have known masks
masks screaming 'bout
being-late-for-my-own-
funeral
masks touching graves
unfolding tomb/wombs,
i have known chalk
masks. clown. stage.
sing-me-a-song
catch-me-again
do-it-again masks
i have known field masks
planting sowing
thirsting masks
known voo-do,
hoo-do-can-i-
git-you masks
Wednesday-torn mask
sing-torn-melodies-
sing-fear-tunes-
wednesday masks
erasing saturday-

morning-full-of-
where-you-been-bitch-blues
i know masks
mother
daughter
sister
wife
masks
peeling
swallowing
leaking
sweating and
running masks
i-have-i-want-to-pain
again masks
buried under
another man
another moon
another woman
mask.
got those
moon masks
full of numbers
full of ripe-time-to-be-
born masks.
i know masks
your masks
midnight i-want-
to-hold-your-name
masks
i know masks

your masks
full of wine
full of love
can-we-
compromise masks
endless
cosmic
poison
demon
MASKS
i have known
i have known
masks.
i have known masks
poet
dancer
music maker
baby maker
masks
full of breath
full of rhythm masks
meet-at-the-same-
time-same-place-
don't-be-late masks.
masks introducing
themselves at breakfast
masks unfolding-their-
wall-street-journal-into-
other-masks. i have
known masks, rich-
college-boy-need-a-

piece,-just-a-piece
masks.
i have known masks
fancy-colored-lady
with-the-starched-
behind MASKS
i have known masks
bus stops
boat stops
plane stops
american docks
japanese motels
nigerian taxicabs
i have known masks
those $45-an-hour-
pour-your-masturbations-out
but-don't-cry masks
those silk-imported-
hand-embroidered-
natural-vegetable-dyed masks
those city masks
those purple-blue-i-want-to-
freak-you masks
i have worn masks
vegetarian
fruitarian
egoist
puritan
eating my masks
torn
worn

face masks
egyptian masks
female
feeding masks
i have worn masks
mother masks
daughter-can-i-teach-
you-now masks
morningtime masks
summertime-in-
carolina masks
baptismal
masks
election-time-
kiss-a-baby's-cheek
masks
i know masks
poet-lady
cry-baby-sitting-on-the-steps masks
MASKS
MASKS
MASKS
MASKS
where-do-you-pack-your-
next-suicide
what-time-does-
the-hurt-stop masks
i know touch masks
i know fear masks
i know love masks
i know birth masks

i know old-brothers-
nodding-on-the-corner masks
i know masks
your masks
train-plane-wherever-we-
meet-again masks
i know masks
saviour masks
regenerative masks
i touch-feel-steal
masks
swallow-
suck-
vomit masks
rich masks
polyester-eat-your-progress-on-your-toast-
in-the-morning masks
memory
masks
old-songs-make-me-cry masks
new-lies-make-me-horny
masks
i know masks
grandma masks
mother-teach-me-the-meaning-of-struggle
masks
those six-o'clock-
see-yourself-murdered-
video masks
those camp-light-
pile-them-high-

burn-them-niggers
masks
masks
masks
masks
Xmas time
gold light masks
sterling silver
mexican
inlaid american-coated
masks
i have known
masks
west coast
sierra
climb-your-ego's-ass-
break-fast
masks.
touch. see. whisper.
nature. season.
honey. butterfly.
seashore masks.
whisper from the ocean
full lady
moon masks
i know masks
Abortion masks
aborted fears
tears smile masks
snapping beans
planting corn

waxing floor
masks
i know masks
geography
world politics
psychology II
education 234-but-niggers-register-w/English-I-
prerequisite masks
Quaker masks
cambodia. plant-a-tree-
earth-day-free-Huey-can-i-wear-
an-Afro-too masks
those sister
strawberry
café
fudge
au chocolait
sweet-talk masks
those jail-house-
visit-at-1:00 Sunday
masks
those bed-time-
love-in-between masks
those masks between your
eyes undressing
my soul
touching-my-life-masks.

I have committed
more suicides than
a Japanese samurai
but softly
softer than Roberta
strumming my
song - spot . . .
softly
like the marbles
nestled in my
plants that refuse
to blanket the water
that freely rinses
their ruby sparkle.
this woman
this child
this birthing
this suicide
unclaimed
hold tightly . . .

Song Of Your Sunday

the white silence
meets me at the last
stop light;
i turn left and
make a rain-washed
yellow almost blinding
right.
you are there
sitting in your
silence
in your damp
meadow of truth.
the sun visits
too but your
eyes are locked
inside my knees.
my thighs quiver
like smoke
and your glare
glistens like
fresh sour
green apples.
wet
green apples.
stolen from
somebody's grandma's tree.
an unripened steal.
the sun spills over your
room, soaking the

mellow rhythms
song of your innermost
seas,
your innermost
rains . . .
be a vine
and travel
through
me
wrapping
and
coiling
my
shadow
like
a smooth
stone.
let me
search
your rooms
and kiss
your nudeness
as I, sun,
weave
into this
ripened sky.
this glistening
this stirring
sunday.

oh, my blood frightened you
when it flowed
and flowed and flows
as you drank with
passion and never
once belched
as you continued to relive
happy days with
your father
beaches, virgins
felt that summer
sun begin
to bake your
small feet/begin to wrinkle
your boy hands
but you drank
w/out ever once
tiring/though you
stared at the blood
at the blood
at this wise
woman blood
I command you shot
at high noon/
        as your hands begin to wrinkle.

look out when a woman stops to think
when she stops and recognizes
that she doesn't recognize
the whispers in her sleep
the wine in her tea
the arms in her bed
when she realizes that this world
is too organized
and too structured for the wisdom of spiders
and gypsy alike.
i have stopped to think about
a woman
a whisper
a drink
a world with arms
an ocean of spider/costumed gypsies
beware this
eight-legged virgin
this cryptic skull w/hieroglyphics
beware these gypsy feet w/bracelets
and rings
and ropes and knives
this is the whispered smile
the bed w/arms
the throat that refuses to snap. . . .

there is always the woman
standing at the back of my
eyes
a very black woman
blacker than all of the oils
of the darkest night
blacker than the fullest of
skies
a black woman holding
back the tears
knotting the curtains of
time. twisting away all
the blood circles
all the dark
black blood
circles that
shadow the cries and
suffocate the
whispers

June 12, 1978

if you can recognize death at birth
or birth at death
i will marry you
wear two veils
sun
moon
black
white
burning. frozen
two veils
two faces
lifting two different cribs
from two different wombs
two veils
blown by two different winds
strangle two necks
separately
tenderly.
a bride to
death
a moon morning
consummation
child calling wind
mother and following
tree shadows that
grow tall like groom-like fathers.

these twisted lips hide a bleeding
heart
hide an apartness . . . a silence
a silence that lapses into explosions
like waterfalls where we once played
        a last silence
        leaves have slept in the earth
        and trees rebirthed where
        i bled upon the soils of this
        ground.
        an old wind still echoes
        still ticks upon this apartness.
        your bronze song is alive
        with eyes blinking out tunes
        and smiles upon the baby child
        unable to see. unable to touch this
        cool earth.
        this song you sing is the uncut
        gem of poetry
        raw autumn candle light
        poetry. i am sun clothed in
        bone and blood
        i am a warning to the birth
        to the sleep to this breath
        of god. only i can celebrate
        your hymn.

for donald —

I.

we bend to pray but instead
fall into each other's arms.
we look out into distances
over twisted bed sheets
have i slept well?
you ask/my eyes tell you
that it is late —
that this is not an hour
i like being awake.
your eyes are black
in the darkening room
the shadow
from the moon
paints your face across my chest —
i smile and your lips move
to cover me — to lick
away the tears/already falling
i hold out my arms to you, though
i'm weak — it's hard resisting
your penetrating warmth.
we awaken and walk among pines
tall, erect, moving brisk
w/morning
their erection is a symbol
of our silence
of our consummable time
of the legacy we leave for remembrance
of the naked place we inherit
in our child — like innocence

II.
breast
distended nipple pouring forth
warmth/flesh
a celebration of solidarity
you sketch my body w/your tongue
slide down to my neck
flow into these shoulders and arms
you fill breasts/nipples
w/love
i expand at your teasing touch
you reshape the borders of my stomach
redefine the outside of legs,
feet, your lips travel up on the inside
brushing my thighs
anointing our morning
restoring our balance.

III.
our lips speak it together
a language repossessed
rediscovered
a new fabric
we create a silkened touch
a new silkened world.
this one night full of moon with
honey tongues
the light
only the light is believable
only the light holds your
face and the ocean's place

where tongues reside
within this other hollow
wet place
within this other hollow place
full of life
full of wet moon seed
honey babies
full of dust
full of earthquake
fire and dance
and tongues
and tongues
and tongues
and oceans
and only the light
only the light
can lead.
this queen
into your silence
into your darkness
a sun mistress
a prayer/touched season.

        i am going out of myself into a womb. into a
skin that breathes, stretches, sheds into a woman
without a mouth. without song. without seed. i am
going into a season w/moon only. w/full moon
stares and full moon shadows. a costume without
player – played out – staged out –
full of memory. song. dance.
slowly i am awakening. lifting veils of ivory
lifting swollen new eyes
lifting white skies
w/prayer
w/wonder
my eyelids mark the calendar
like crickets that know the season
for mating
that know the season
for song
i have new rhythms
that pulsate earth
that hold on to autumn freedom
i have new rhythms
unaltered
i am a new season
with reason
on the edge of a scream
on the edge of my soul
turning illusions inside out
i am going out of myself
running away to a new twilight
a twilight prism
faceted

w/truth
w/fear
w/rebirth
where light is too bright
grass too green
skies too perfect
this summer bed
is a dream
creased w/fantasy
language is all a lie
words cannot stretch
this earth
cannot feed this new rainbow
cannot trace God's colors.
when i curl back into winter
only the stars hear
when i form clusters
hang full
ripened
sunlit
only the stars hear
from spring to winter
i will probe this rich bowl
become full
hang low
stretch into old stories
old lace
old letters
i am going out of myself
into history
to wander in rooms of pink

gold
palest green
to shine in newness
to shine in birth
in death
into history
breathing the goldness of –
old stories
old women
old heartaches
old freedom
new bondage
the palest green
deepens
i too become
new ripe
seasoned
thrust
propelled w/light
yielding continents
a magnet to this spiritual eclipse

self portrait:over-exposed

Hey Lady

    w/verse between

    your teeth and

    rhythm disguised as wax

    becoming loose in your ears

        Hey Lady

        Poem Lady w/

an evil way w/word roots

you be planting

ju-ju and goobah dust

inside my moon thighs

        Hey Circle Woman

coming this way again

riding on cowrie shells and the shadow

of a thousand Egun-gun.

I.
I don't see you often
though your face
is reflected upon the
autumn leaves
I know springs
I know summers
falls
and winters
and I remember
having known you
in the autumn
when days are golden and warm
I remember winter
when hot chocolate spilled
all over your new leather coat
and I laughed
when you screamed
Oh shit!
and then there is summer
I will always
remember
picnic baskets
and wine
and wine
and wine
and tears
and good bread
good cheese
good fruit

I must remember
long-stemmed roses
you used to buy for me
and I too used to buy for you.
I most remember.

II.
One winter night that was cold
you were cold when you said
I can't see you anymore
and suddenly my coat
fell open
and winter rushed in
possessed my bones
my soul
my very being
and I laughed. Almost stumbled
as you drew me near
looked into my eyes
now brimming with tears
and you said in a whisper
she knows. . . .
I coughed and whispered back
    she knows?
She knows, I kept whispering
all the way home, or did I
go home?
I asked the white line on the
highway —
she knows?
I asked· the car whose path
I was headed straight into
she knows?

III.
lying in a cold room with strange
white hands massaging
my neck or head
I asked

she knows?

Jaki, do you know why
you're here, the handsome
black doctor asked
(in my head, I kept saying
I know him from somewhere,
I know this doctor but I don't
remember from where
probably met him
at a party

No. I whispered.
do you remember what happened?
the starched face of the
white girl psychiatrist
smiled a pancake smile
and said – Jaki, I'm going
to try and help you to
remember
(how can she help me I
thought)
she proceeds to ask me
what planet I live on
and do I believe there are

alien beings here trying
to possess me
I answered to her that I
too am a student of
analytical reasoning and
to go fuck HER analyst
the black doctor takes my
hand and quietly tells me
I've attempted suicide . . .
my stomach has been pumped
and I will probably
feel groggy for a little while.

(I remember where I
met the doctor)
Oh! you are a friend
of Jesselyn's husband
remember, I'm her poet
friend. I met you
at a cocktail party
there last month.
remember you stared at my
cleavage all night
while your rich and ugly Liberian —
turned — american white girl — wife
bragged about HER monetary assets

Oh god I've embarrassed him
he knows this depressed
psychotic suicidal woman

IV.

I am wheeled out to you in the
waiting room. Your eyes are all
red —
you stand
go get the car
tuck me into the passenger's seat
silence takes over
you look at me with tears
and say —
I can't see you anymore
I can't bear holding you in my
arms as you silently slip away.

V.

I cry hard
I swallow the very last of my
forty valium
      (nine to be exact)
and pray that the stop light
never changes to green
that we never move forth
      anymore.

the wind blows
like halloween
and your sleepy eyes
whisper
that —
summer is almost over
the walls shiver
w/my breath
this pungent poet breath
writing
singing
dancing breath
the trees
dance a minuet
across the ceiling
our arms stretch
out —
into cathedrals
your heart
begins
its pilgrimage
becoming a pincushion
for my
dreamless
shadowless
dramas
my tears
my birth fears
my morning time fears.
I sing a song of wifehood
to the walls

to the winds
to the trees
to the children sleeping
to the children sprouting
I sing a long winter song
of love,
snow drift cascading upon
erect breasts
these breasts
these temples of redemption
upon your brow
upon your springtime
my womb opens into the palace
of reds
into the palace
of spiraling
magical feats and moon tunes.
our season
our child in flight
I am full
intoxicated
w/your smile
your touch
your smell
I wade dreamily
silently —— into – your river's womb.

regret

today we sat against
a brick wall —
on damp leaves
facing the sun
we ate
salami
pumpernickel
played with the bees
today
was a good day
for cheese
wine
holding hands
only
I wasn't happy
because
this place belonged
to another time
w/another man
this was my secret place
but today —
I opened the circle
decided to share
w/you.
it was hard to roll in the leaves
w/you.
because the leaves
knew me, knew my touch.
knew the touch of

another man/w me
it was hard
even though
the sun was warm
against my back
the leaves were like
a velvety cushion
for our frolics
but
I knew I made a mistake
when up popped a branch
reaching out
tripping me
I violated my secret
my pact w/this love forest.

1

these lonely tear smiles
broad with silence
broad with childhood pain
pulsating
above this flower head
above this night element
growing dark
with smoke from the forest
this blinding tear smile
of love
of memory
of unforgettable thunder
love elements
black gold
rumbling
black gold forest
dust
gold dust
night gold

2
all day
touch

3
I walk towards
your madness
your dance
scorches
my breast

4
forest spirit
black gold
forest/spirit
scream

5
vanish

6
thumb through
your childhood belly
thumb through
black gold
forest womb

7
all day
rest
touch
crush
breast
gold/black
breast
drip
into
gold/black
milk/tears

All praise be the name

the tongues of this
womb — voice
sing my mother's
birth song
sing her laboring cries
sing and cry
praises to her heavy breathing
creating self
this womb voice
melodic
wind caught
fire teased
so close to birth
so close to closing night
these tongues
teased by slavery
teased by freedom
teased by life air
these tongues
full of gold dust
casting
Egyptian
womb tombs . . .
that an eager wind has blown
is not important
that a stormy tuesday night
sings
the blues too loudly
is my only testament

i sing into deaf cups
shower myself
among my own ghosts
as I collect
my aggressions
I understand the connection
the umbilicus
of my tears
to my blood.

to young white boys who don't know what they be getting into . . .

I will give you this continent
this vast dark map of soulful mystery
tastes and tongues and the parting of curves,
waves and dancing hips
your mouth stands erect
at each natural shore
erect
to receive the darkness
that
has bathed you
fed you
and even loved you in your white age
of growing up

distance
a crucifix trapped in your
throat
suppressing your roar of lust
for black Sahara breasts
whispering to uncircumcised deserts
whispering to the downpours of your adolescence

you are your own man

i have forgotten
what you looked like
as a free man
i don't hear the free songs
of your rambling spirit
even your echoes seem harnessed
and your shadow wears
a hangman's noose

Background music: Fireworks cheering

Thursday Jan. 11 11/354

8 the simmering of blood

9 the simmering of blood.

10 the simmering of blood. the simmering

11 of blood. the simmering of blood the

12 simmering of blood. THE SIMMERING OF BLOOD. the simmering of blood. the simmering of blood. The simmering of blood.

evening

Friday Jan. 12 12/353

8 blood the simmering of blood the simmering

9 of blood of blood of blood of blood

10

11

the simmering of blood the simmering of blood the simmering of blood the simmering of blood

Happy 4th of July

evening

Saturday Jan. 13 13/352

THE SIMMERING of blood.
The simmering of blood.
The simmering of blood
the simmering of blood

Sunday Jan. 14 14/351

the simmering of blood the simmering of blood
the simmering of blood the simmering of blood
the simmering of blood the simmering of blood
the simmering of blood the simmering of blood

AT-A-GLANCE®

Lifting my veil
is easy
if done in December
or perhaps September
but never April
but never July
never when the time
is wet, warm, full of
seed.
lift my veil
my eyes whimper
but close
my eyes moan
but cling to the word
Season. cold. dry.
fold back the moon veil and step
aside for whispers
for words.

For Mary

your calmness was haunting
i could not say as some
have said that you only
looked asleep.
   you looked dead
   with a plastic anchor
launched from your nostrils
trying to anchor back to
your world
     of reefer-teased summer
your world of musk
          funk
          and spoiled nights
you still only look dead
as i cry tears that are sour
that are too short
but sting too heavily.

i must send you away
where other mothers go
to know peace
and only the sweet silence of children's smiles
as they cascade across your deadness. Your finality.

your stomach was full of death
pregnant, big with dead blood
Real death . . .
We salute your motherhood
sisterhood
wifehood
maidenhead w/southern
succulence
w/ anointed feeling of femaleness.

112

your daughters sing life songs
sing morning blues about
their mother done gone
done forgot how to
smile to the morning
and curse the night
your sons shoot blind bullets
shoot with crooked arrows
that spiral and ricochet
across your new grave
your new bed place
sleeping place w/clay quilts
that keep out the day
and perish the night

you are loosening your hold
my thread soul
ravels

urging me to pass through
myself, to stop and feel this
black empty patient throbbings
of boredom with freedom
and curiosity left naked
tall with the smell
of maleness
and dead winter seed.
Shall i murder you
swallow you in order
to tame you
in order to satisfy
my pretending when i am
sick of death and awakening
to beautiful strangers who
have become fruit
inside this ball
this raveling delicious thread ball raveling all
over your navel
your body smoke
cloudy dense w/ moon rain
smells like burning cloth
like skin being boiled
trying to hide the blood
the name in the blood
the name in the fire
the unmarked name being

boiled alive in moon rain
collected from your thread cloth
thick but never fades
the name speaks of
rivers and graves without
identification, the wanderer
walking at night whose cheek
is kissed with moon rain
and scorched with sun.

wind and morning sweat
escort me
down the street,
past the older sisters
on the uptown side
waiting
to go clean
somebody's house
waiting
to go to some
fretful
dying
matron of cancer.
I pass
sometimes
open-eyed
with smiles
sometimes dense
with the tease
of cocaine
piercing
lungs
sometimes
with camera
trying
to steal
lock
their shadows
inside my eyes

I am preparing
to meet
a strange face
a stranger
who —
when summer
skies return
will lead
my bursting
desires
to a golden river.
preparing to be
pierced. consumed
preparing to be
tamed. executed
by the wind.
strange face
stands in line
prisoner thirty-seven
must never speak
in whispers again
terror in the wind
sends
out
circular
light
dark oils
burn
turn
into
cold
sand

you can even
get lost
at home
inside
your own home
your own ice
ask how
so much smoke
got in your
bed.
put the baby
beside the breast
and the violin
into the cradle
and spread
your
winter bread
on the table
prepare
prepare
to kiss
to chase
the straw
the bleeding
nymph's daughter
prepare
to escort
your sinking
lonely
soul
to bed.

in the light upon the center of the sinking room

four almost frozen
almost golden
almost white
almost exact
almost born
almost dead
in the light upon the center of the
sinking room
four almost
empty hands
form speech
form unmeasurable
shadows and snatch
the last bit
of veiled darkness
four empty hands
beginning to rise
from sleep
beginning to call out
from behind
painted lips
denial?
there is surrender in
everything
there is peace in
everything
that wears a crown.
that knows how to love
that knows how to share
the terrible eyes of sleep.

HIPS

Hips
Hips
Hips w/bracelets of alligator teeth
python bells
hips undulated w/pheremone
hips w/african flavor
encasing your breath
your screams
hips laced w/wine
painted red. blue. browns
painted w/earth flesh
hips
choking your video fantasies
hips
black
brown
circles of hips
wading in the water
climbing mountains
hips
kneeling
praying
reaching
hips
nursing african civilizations
hips
enveloping
nations
black hips

sun baked
hips
planting
praying
aborting cancer
aborting ameriKKKa
hips swaying
under magnolia
limbs
hips
protecting
life
from
ropes
from
bullets
from poison
wombs
hips
sweet
round
strong
nation
hips
national
freedom
hips
hips
hips
these hips
painted

w/moon sweat
these full
virgin
hips
these
bridal
hips
carving
life before altars
these
mother
hips
these
hips
shaped
like
bowls
like
cups
like
vessels
these
pouring
spilling
swelling
authentic
natural
motherland
hips
hips
shaping

earth
into
babies
shaping
weeds
into
food
shaping
branches
into
knives
these
hips
aquiline
piercing
these
hips
of
purpose
hips
hips
hips
inherited
matriarchal
broad
like
breasts
hips
hips
with
crooked

eyes
seeing
sleeping
shifting
staring
hips
naked
w/silk
w/honey
w/cosmic nectar
w/virgin sweat

PART IV

To my grandmother
and Martin Luther King, Jr.

EVA I

the last Sunday
i remember you
in hat
pastels
soft gray hair posing beneath
your HATNESS
(only black women achieve the HAT-NESS)
that i envy you for.
You —
    grandmother
    African Methodist Episcopal
    Missionary
    Widowed minister's wife
    Mother of four
    grandmother of five
    great grandmother of fourteen
    HAT-NESS IS INHERITED
    it's in the blood
    because i got the Hatness
    too —
        i can put on your
        old silk and taffeta and
        linen dresses, petticoats and
        suits — and top this little
        head w/a panama
        and hatness becomes herstorical
        enriched w/Her/Your/Our style.

EVA II

the lord is my shepherd
i shall not want . . .

Does the shepherd have a wife
loving hands forming clouds
little creatures
centipedes and dust
loving hands forming rainbows
in grandchildren's eyes
does the shepherd have a soul-mate
earth rain in white hair
strength shining through a neon halo . . . a neon archer
the shepherd has a house
her pillars bronze aztec
centuries of egyptian snuff
in this golden vessel
consumed into this deposit of
civilization, this deposit in a shepherd land.

EVA III

your thunderbolts follow us still
the old oak tree in the path
stands. still. its seams healed
now —
we no longer use it as a clothes line
success requires a dryer
and never clothes hanging in the background
on Sunday
ain't success a bitch
central harlem drive
haunts this granddaughter
where the poetess tries to create
sonatas with air
a hudson river angel repossessed
by these longfellow avenue
riverside drive skeletons
ah — these thunderbolts
this prison-population explosion
this rain dripping blood
drowning our thunderbolts
our sunday morning smiles
your mission to deliver thunder
in small drinks.

for grandmother —

        if you could know how much i missed you. so many nights. hurt. crying.
wanting you again. wanting to tell you how much your strength, your history,
your life has touched my life. given me strength. helped me to grow
hoping i am a granddaughter you can be proud of. oh — how I remember
all sorts of details, all sorts of ideas you planted within me. I have
wondered about your fantasies, your dreams, your fears, I know you
feared death and knew that we would have won that battle with
death if you had been home — if you could have heard little
feet and screams and toy cash registers, toy telephones being
slammed and dragged across the floor — if you could have heard the
too loud disco music from your great granddaughter's room
and my car screeching into the backyard, if you had heard
we would have beat death. you died with your quilt — your quilt
handmade by your hands — loving hands that have bathed babies
snapped the necks of chickens, dug for earthworms and grubs
loving hands that have plaited hair and hemmed skirts, dresses
and always grasping — holding — clutching. hands that touched my legs
on a brisk sunday morning to see if I were wearing stockings, hands
that have washed floors and soothed backs. loving hands. sweaty
sometimes but never cold. always warm and powerful.
creation, grandma — is a continuum, and by an act of grace we are
driven to enter into it, even when we feel we are weak — without seed. we are
given. there are days when i forget how important my lone days are —
how important it is at times like this not to fulfill anything — only to
lie awake — thinking — i am learning to let me rest, occasionally,
to learn the path of a wanderer, to live only for the room — for the
shadows — the light becomes evening and leaves me like a lover
stealing back a love poem. at times like these i want to be —
need to be whatever. at times like these. i feel no grace. no elegance.
what i am learning as an adult, grandma — about love, about marriage,
about fruitful lives — commitment. hunger for stability — harmony —
my growth wilts without these — my growth wants experience.
life and love with me are expanding with my age. sex, these days
seems so unimportant yet it does enlarge my own self consciousness —
my new-found body languages.
sometimes i feel — without taste — such is loneliness — i feel dead — i need
to hurt/it arouses me, reminds me to swallow but never taste.
boredom and panic seem to play tic-tac-toe often with me.
panic — afraid to live
            afraid to be nourished.
            afraid to create.

A birthday tribute I

my grandmother
Martin
probably/perhaps
was like your grandmother
bronze
high cheekbones
elongated
sculptured neck
pewter hair
an incredible carriage
always erect
poised
ready to succumb
eager to strike
eager to seek rest
peace
my grandmother
like
your grandmother
held your pride
your bleeding nose
your splintered chest
inside/her dirty apron pockets
held your head
your brains
under the heirloom quilt
wove
your words
your whispers

your prayers
into curtains/
hung them high
my grandmother
like
your grandmother
would bathe in your tears
cleanse your wounds w/the milk of her nativity
cleanse your heart w/the honey of her offspring
grandmothers, Martin
knew how to do the do
to hold back the night
to stand in line when the line was a curve
with torches in the middle —
grandmothers, Martin
bore your limbs
her teeth holding up your manhood
teeth mother
clenching tradition
and engulfing its shadow —
you are the dream
of their stolen nights
the gardens
the cotton fields
the plowing —
fresh
at the end of a weary day
you made the six mile walks over
snake strewn paths
to the white lady's house
to pick up dirty laundry

to seem necessary
) take laundry back six miles
again
through forest
over bridges
dust
heat
wash
dry
starch
iron
fold
reload basket –
carry it back again
you turned the fifty cents
into ethiopian treasure –
you made the walk
a crusade
a carousing
a sweet tiredness
you gave them purpose –
Martin
my grandmother/your grandmother
i know they were alike
Sunday mornings
blue felt hats w/satin birds
ostrich feathers
they carried little red bibles
missionaries
quiet
humming

watching little boys like you
become men
become warriors
become statues
landmarks
historical footnotes
they were so alike
holding and sharing
the pain of granddaughters —
losing sons, Martin
tears
letting go of the holy ghost
feasting at the love
table
early sunrise
prayer services
they link a great
circle
Martin
they climbed with you
we follow.

A birthday tribute II

There were no poets there, none,
standing beside your crib
no firethrowers, no lights
but your mother knew
she felt this Shango-child
that she had birthed
your fetal movements were
little echoes of boom, boom, boom
marching
little spears demanding
the wind to speak
there were no poets there
Martin
when you arrived — but
your mother's birth pains
were sonnets
sonatas, lyrical, whispering
a far away drum rhythm
no poets
but your mother's blood
flowing
into your veins
your muscles
created another song
a loud freedom hymnal
and angels gathered in georgia too
winged you
birthed you
your memories of black faces

fire flies
clay dirt
mountains
your memories
trails of childhood
trails of history
no poets
from Selma to Alabama
but your blood
always rhymed w/mine
no poets
hiding under dingy sheets
but their bullets
were fierce
alliteration
no poets
Martin
when you climbed the mountain
but when you echoed
we answered back
from the valley
as poets
in harmony
forceful
as only your poem of life could be.

A birthday tribute III

Martin
you are a master light
a black cat
jumping out of freedom's coffin
floating
crossing slavery's path
you are a master light
spirit glowing
spirit shouting
a master light
turning nights deep red
deep red
is the color of freedom
brilliant
burning
pulling the strings
of your own spiritual universe
you are deep red screams
loud –
you are a man
who is loud
on the birth
of his ways
you redefine lives
souls
predict their worlds
your song is heard
your sun rays chime
your coming

A birthday tribute IV

The calling

your song god awoke you from
slumber
your song-god
called you
put a cow's tail in your hand
asked you to sing
but you knew no songs
Martin,
but your song-god urged you
to sing for your grandfathers
and for your fathers and for
the sake of your house
and so, you did and from then and
until now
your mouth is
full of songs;
not good songs, not sweet
songs — not yet
then one day
the song-god returned
and this time,
he puts a horse's tail, a large, beautiful
shining horse's tail in your hand
a golden voice to sing
and you sing powerful songs

screams
blossoms
buds
fulfills young black seed
nourishes old black souls
freedom's coffin is sweet
no surprises
only smiling
stars
you are a
master light
spirit glowing
spirit shouting
spirit burning

songs that caused the dead
to come alive
songs that evoked the spirit
of the ancestors
i too shall be strong
and my voice
shall be
strong —
my song-god!
My Martin
can you hear me
Martin
where are you?

Revelations

an old woman in me awakens patiently
i was born in 1829
late in the afternoon
the last red leaves were raping the trees
there was a full moon
the Grannies in the cabins
kept a watchful eye on me
told me tales of how someday
Truth
would set me free
free
in the elegance of African blood
blood sister
that knows the secret place
behind the heart
the secret place
beneath the veins
where the moon hides a dream –
an old woman in me walks patiently
we evaporate into wind
smear blood over our thick
red lips
we smear blood under our African breasts
it is our baptism
our commitment
to each other's souls
from this day forth
we are locked in blood
blood sister

that knows the secret place behind the heart
the light shines through us
blood sisters
glorious red
glorious black
we are a cage of crystals
in the sun
our Blackness
our Africanness
more beautiful than the darkness
of imagination
i worship the light that pumps
your heart
i worship the dream you appear in
blood sister
old woman
tender
proud
fragments of myself
fragments of history . . .

for grandma

I heard your voice this morning
speaking from the foot of the bed
your quilt crawled to the
floor
as I lay down in the
first whisper of dawn.
I heard your voice this morning
the sound of cloth
a casual sound
a sunday morning
preparing to visit your lord
sound
half your life
half my life
half my daughter's life
we all dream of landscapes
romantic deserts
white sands
connecting us together.
a half dozen roses
I play out my life
listening every morning
for your voice
at the foot of the bed.

Jaki Shelton Green

Jaki Shelton Green is a community activist and writer. She has worked as an Arts and Education Consultant and as a Community Economic Development Consultant. She is working on a Juke Joint project which is partially funded by the North Carolina Arts Council. She has performed her poetry and taught workshops in the United States, the Caribbean, Europe, and Brazil.

Jaki Shelton Green's poetry has appeared in textbooks, journals, anthologies, and publications such as the *Crucible*, *The African-American Review*, *Essence* magazine and *Obsidian*. Her works include *conjure blues*, *Dead on Arrival*, *Dead on Arrival and New Poems*, *Masks*, and *Blue Opal*, a play. She is a contributing author to *Pete and Shirley: The Great Tar Heel Novel*, and is completing a collection of short stories.

Designed at Bull City Studios,
Durham, North Carolina.

Printed in an edition of one thousand by
Braun-Brumfield, Inc,,
Ann Arbor. Michigan.